Anonymous

**Grand Forks, the Metropolis of the Red River Valley**

Its commerce, manufactures, and progress

Anonymous

**Grand Forks, the Metropolis of the Red River Valley**
*Its commerce, manufactures, and progress*

ISBN/EAN: 9783337290696

Printed in Europe, USA, Canada, Australia, Japan

Cover: Foto ©Suzi / pixelio.de

More available books at **www.hansebooks.com**

# Metropolis of the Red River Valley

———ITS———

# Commerce, Manufactures

# AND PROGRESS

Saint Paul
Northwestern Publishing Company
1882

# GRAND FORKS,

## DAKOTA.

Northwestern Publishing Co.
Printers, Publishers & Lithographers,
St. Paul, Minn.

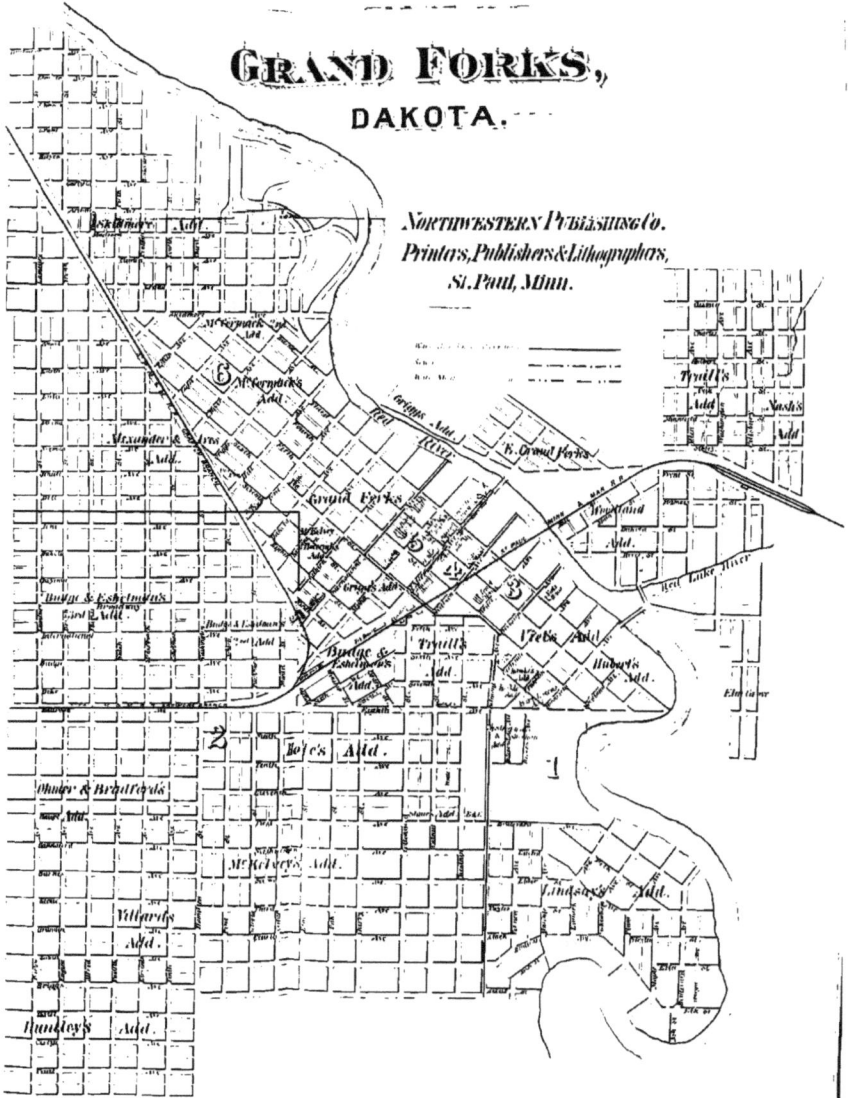

Skidmore Add.

McCormack 2nd Add.

McCormack's Add.

Alexander & Ayres Add.

Griggs Add.

Grand Forks

E. Grand Forks

Tryill's Add.

Nash's Add.

Woodland Add.

Red Lake River

Budge & Eshelman's First Add.

Budge & Eshelman's Add.

Budge & Eshelman's Add.

Tryill's Add.

Viets Add.

Hubert's Add.

Elevator

Boye's Add.

Ohmer & Bradfords Add.

McKelvey's Add.

Lindsay's Add.

Villards Add.

Huntley's Add.

# PREFACE.

The statistics and historical and biographical information contained in this work have been carefully collected and compiled with a view of giving a true and accurate description of Grand Forks, its past history, present condition, and future prospects.

Particular attention is called to the accompanying map, which was lithographed from exact copies of the plats on record in the register of deeds' office for Grand Forks. The copies were made by one of the most prominent surveyors of that city, a gentleman whose connection with the work is a positive guaranty of its accuracy.

The publishers are glad to be able to present the citizens of Grand Forks with a work which it is hoped will be found, in every respect, worthy of the very liberal support which it has received, and they desire to say that the unavoidable delay in its publication has been caused solely by their desire to have it, as nearly as possible, perfect.

THE PUBLISHERS.

## NOTICE.

Copies of this work and of similar publications, descriptive of Moorhead and Crookston, Minnesota, and Jamestown and Valley City, Dakota, may be obtained at the rate of 50 cents for each work, by addressing

Northwestern Publishing Company,

(Box 2258,)                                               Saint Paul.

# Grand Forks

Brief Sketch of the History of Dakota and the Red River Valley

## THE SOIL, CLIMATE AND AGRICULTURAL ADVANTAGES— SPLENDID COMMERCIAL AND INDUSTRIAL POSITION OF GRAND FORKS—DESCRIPTION OF THE CITY, ETC., ETC.

A glance at the map of the United States will show the reader the very important position that Dakota occupies, relative to the other sections of the Union. From the British provinces on the north it stretches by a succession of beautiful and fertile prairies to the state of Nebraska on the south. On the east is Minnesota, rapidly becoming one of our most important and influential commonwealths, while to the west lie the territories of Montana and Wyoming, with their immense deposits of valuable metals and minerals. When to this unexcelled geographical position is added the fact that Dakota embraces a territory estimated at 149,100 square miles, or 95,424,000 acres, it will be seen what a splendid future she has before her. Figures so vast are not easily grasped by the mind, and our readers may perhaps better understand the size of this territory by comparison with some of the Eastern states and foreign countries. Pennsylvania, for instance, contains 45,215 square miles and New York 49,170, so that each of them is less than one-third the size of Dakota. Great Britain and Ireland together are 27,000 square miles smaller than this territory, and Italy only a little over two-thirds as large.

When it is remembered that all this vast region is susceptible of cultivation; that its population has risen from 14,181 in 1870 to nearly a quar-

(3)

ter of a million to-day; that numerous towns and cities, future centers of commercial and industrial activity, are springing up on all sides,—when all this is remembered, it will be seen that we do not exaggerate in saying that Dakota is undoubtedly destined to occupy in the near future a position politically, agriculturally, and commercially inferior to none of the older states.

Although Dakota as a whole is so remarkably fertile and productive, there are sections which are particularly notable, the more so that they are the best among so much that is good.

### THE RED RIVER VALLEY

is the chosen region *par excellence* of the farmer, a region unexcelled by any on the face of the earth for the surpassing fertility of the soil and the wonderful crops, especially of wheat, which it produces.

### THE RED RIVER

has its source in Big Stone Lake, in the county of the same name, Minnesota, and flowing north by a winding and circuitous route, empties into Lake Winnepeg, in the British province of Manitoba.

The length of the valley from Big Stone Lake to Lake Winnepeg is about 300 miles, while its breadth is about 100 miles. The whole of this vast section was at one time completely under water, forming the bed of an immense lake, which, when it dried up and disappeared, left behind it a deposit of rich mud—the present soil of the valley.

The following, from the pen of Professor Denton, of Massachusetts, published originally in the *Duluth Tribune*, is one of the best and most lucid explanations ever attempted of the wonderful geological changes that took place in this region at the close of the glacial period:

"When the cold of the glacial period gave place to the present climate, the indications are that the change took place instantaneously, and the great ice sheet then covering this northern region—in some places a mile or more in thickness—was" (by a new inclination of the earth's axis to the plane of its orbit) "suddenly introduced to a temperate climate. Melting in the hot summer suns, it produced a flood, the effects of which are observable to the geologist from North Minnesota to the Gulf. But such a body of ice melted not in one or a dozen summers. For many years lay the great ice field to the north, preventing the passage of waters in the direction the general slope of the country here would have led them, and thus, as far south as the slope of the land would permit, a lake existed where the Red River Valley now is, and gradually enlarged to the north as the ice melted. At the bottom of the lake mud was continually being deposited, produced by the ground-down Silurian, Devonian, and Cretaceous beds lying to the north, over which the ice still for many years continued to move, bearing masses of their earthy substances. When it was all melted the dammed-up waters found a natural outlet to Hudson's Bay, and the Red river was formed. Thus in the Red River Valley the glacial drift—boulders, gravel, etc.—is covered deep beneath the lake mud, and that mud is now the soil of the country, admirably adapted to the production of grain best fitted to build up the physical system of man."

Favored with a soil so exceptionally adapted to cropping, especially of the King Cereal, the farmers of the Red River Valley have succeeded in producing a quality of spring wheat which has not its equal in the world for milling purpose. This is

THE FAMOUS NO. 1 HARD,

of which the celebrated Minnesota flour is made, a flour which commands the highest prices in all the marts of commerce. So deep are these rich deposits of fertile loam (from 24 to 30 inches, with a splendid clay subsoil) that they are practically inexhaustible, and wheat has been grown yearly in the same soil, in the neighborhood of the present city of Winnipeg, for over 50 years.

Before dismissing the subject of the agricultural advantages of the Red River Valley, we must say a word on that most important point,

THE CLIMATE,

as a matter very intimately connected with the successful conducting of all farming operations. Persons who have never passed a winter in Minnesota or Dakota are generally of the impression that the climate is intensely cold—a perfect Artic winter—almost unbearable by either man or beast. Never was an opinion more erroneous or less sustained by facts. That the climate of the Northwest is not as mild as the climate of Florida no one denies, but that it is far more healthy is indisputable. Instead of the damp, wet atmosphere of the Eastern and Middle states, causing pulmonary diseases of all kinds, the Northwest has dry, clear, bracing weather, and the cold is not near as perceptible as in sections where the thermometer scarcely ever reaches zero. During the winter of '81–'82, the coldest month, January, had a mean temperature of 5.5 degrees, while December's average was 20.3 degrees, and February's 16.7. These figures are from the United States Signal Service at Moorhead, and their accuracy can be relied on.

It may perhaps be thought that we have devoted too much space to Dakota and the Red River Valley in general, to the detriment of what is more particularly the subject of this work,

### THE CITY OF GRAND FORKS.

But it should be remembered that it is on the country that cities depend for their business and support, especially in a new country like this, whose manufacturing interests are as yet comparatively undeveloped. If the surrounding country is rich, and the agricultural community numerous and prosperous, business in the towns is sure to be lively, and the merchants contented and happy. This is exactly the position of Grand Forks, for rapid as has been her growth and development, enormous as have been the improvements that she has made in every particular during the past two or three years, the country has outgrown the city, and we doubt if there is a merchant or business man who is not doing a large and satisfactory trade.

The name, Grand Forks, is derived from the fact that the city is located at the junction of the Red River and one of its most important branches, the Red Lake River.

Both of these streams are navigable, the former as far up as Fargo and Moorhead, 80 miles distant from the Forks by rail, and the latter to Crookston. Regular lines of steamboats ply between Fargo and Winnipeg, calling at Grand Forks during the summer season, and large quantities of freight are shipped by this cheap and convenient route. The rivers also afford an invaluable water-way for the transportation of millions of feet of lumber, which are floated down from the immense pineries of Minnesota to the various saw-mills along their borders, where they are speedily utilized in building the happy homes of the emigrant and new settler. Some idea of the importance of this lumbering industry may be formed from the fact that the "drive" of last year was over 3,000,000 feet, while this year it will reach 7,000,000, and perhaps more. The borders of the rivers in the neighborhood of the city are heavily wooded, and fuel, that great requisite of a prairie country, is to be had at from $2 to $3 per cord.

### THE EARLY HISTORY

of Grand Forks dates back no further than the year 1869, when Captain Griggs, of the firm of Hill, Griggs & Co., in company with Captain McCormick, the present mayor of the city, built a rude log hut, the first building

\

erected by white men within the limits of the present city. The Red River Valley was at that time comparatively unknown, except to a few hardy frontiersmen, who, ever on the alert to discover favorable commercial points, had pushed out far beyond the then limits of civilization. The Northern Pacific the pioneer north-western railroad, had not as yet commenced track-laying, and three years were to elapse before it should reach the Red river, at Moorhead. The St. Paul & Pacific, (now the St. Paul, Minneapolis & Manitoba,) the management of which was originally connected with the Northern Pacific, though nominally a separate company, did not lay its tracks on the east side of the Red River until 1872, so that in winter, when the stream was frozen, all the supplies needed by the pioneers of Grand Forks had to be hauled by teams for long distances. The trials and vicis-situdes of these early settlers would have completely discouraged men less resolute than Captain McCormick and his companions, but they were of that material of which the true western pioneer is made, and were men who knew no such word as fail.

In 1873, very shortly after the St. Paul & Pacific had reached Crookston, the nearest railroad town to the Forks, the great financial panic, precipitated by the heavy failure of Jay Cooke & Co., and the suspension of all building operations on the Northern Pacific, occurred, and for over two years, until 1875, the whole Northwest was in a state of complete business inactivity. Emigration ceased, and numbers left the country, returning to their former homes in the eastern states.

When the panic of 1873 occurred, the population of Grand Forks did not exceed half a hundred, and the general merchandise store of Griggs, Walsh & Co. was the sole representative of the commercial interests of the town; forming, with a saw-mill and boat-yard, the entire business establishments of Grand Forks.

In 1874 the Hudson Bay Company, having bought the pioneer mill and store, proceeded to erect the Northwestern Hotel and a new store, which, notwithstanding the terrible depression in business all over the country, and especially in the Northwest, started a small building boom, which continued throughout the year, adding several new houses and stores, and attracting a few new settlers. In 1875 the business outlook commenced to brighten, though very slowly, and construction was recommenced on the St. Paul & Pacific Railroad, under a new management, who changed its name to the St. Paul, Minneapolis & Manitoba Company. Mr. J. J. Hill was the master-mind who directed the fortunes of the new organization, and who has pushed on, overcoming all obstacles, until to-day his railroad ranks as a prosperous, paying investment with any other road in the country.

The line of the railroad, however, passed through Crookston, 26 miles distant from Grand Forks, and it was necessary that she should build her own railroad to the former city, if she desired to fully benefit by the proximity of the great trunk line. Accordingly a number of enterprising gentlemen, forming the Red River Transportation Company, undertook the construction of this short line, and on October 1, 1875, the whistle of the locomotive was first heard in Grand Forks. Although the completion of all rail communication, via Crookston, was an important event in the commercial history of this city, yet it was soon evident that a direct line was an absolute necessity if the interests and growth of the place were to be fully developed. The Manitoba Company accordingly, in 1879, commenced the construction of their line from Fargo to Grand Forks, and the first regular train passed over the new road on January 1, 1880. The population had now increased until it numbered nearly 1,200, and numerous stores and dwellings had been erected on all sides. When six months later, in June, the United States census was taken, 1,800 persons were returned as residents of the city, while the population of Grand Forks county was 6,248. The vote of the county, which at the election for congressional delegate, in 1878, had been 370 for the Republican candidate to 308 for the Democratic, was, in 1880, 604 Republican and 888 Democratic votes.

Since 1880 the growth of Grand Forks has been phenominally great. Hundreds have come from almost every state in the Union, and Europe and Canada are largely represented by the thrifty and industrious Scandinavian, German, and Irish, and the enterprising Canadian. New stores, devoted to almost every branch of business, have been opened, manufacturing establishments started, and a trade already amounting to millions has been built up. Although as yet this trade is almost entirely retail, yet several of the largest houses are acquiring a jobbing business, and the numerous thriving towns and settlements which dot the country in every direction, and whose natural wholesale depot is undoubtedly Grand Forks, leave no room for doubt that this city will become in the near future an important wholesale market.

### THE PRESENT CONDITION OF GRAND FORKS

could not be more favorable to its continued growth and prosperity. New enterprises are continually being started by men of large capital and long business experience, whose connection with a business is a positive guaranty of its success.

The location of the city on the banks of the Red river affords, as we have already said, a cheap means of transportation for freight either south to Fargo and the Northern Pacific, or north to Winnipeg and the Canadian Pacific. The enterprising citizens are not, however, satisfied with a single water route, and they propose to build, in connection with the citizens of Duluth, a canal which will connect the two cities, and afford a cheap means of transportation for the immense crops of the Red River Valley to the Eastern states, via Duluth and the great lakes. The advantages which will at once accrue to the whole Northwest when this canal is completed are too evident to need any elaborate explanation. Freightage by rail is necessarily more costly than by water, and this cost is not unfrequently increased far above its legitimate figure by the demands of railroads in sections where they have no competition, or are not led by a pooling arrangement to entirely control the carrying business.

The surest and easiest way to obviate a monopoly of this character is undoubtedly to construct canals wherever practicable—a truth which the people of the Northwest have, with their usual foresight, been quick to appreciate.

The distance from Duluth to Grand Forks is 380 miles; but the number of navigable rivers and lakes, and natural water-ways, lying between the two cities, reduce the distance over which it would require a canal to be constructed to less than 40 miles, and the entire cost, including dams and locks, to $4,000,000. The Red River and its tributary streams furnish 4,000 miles of navigable waters, and the extent of territory that would benefit by the construction of this canal is immense, not only in its extent, but in the vast crops which it annually yields. Eastern capital is largely interested in the enterprise, and five years will undoubtedly see this splendid work accomplished.

Next in importance to the canal are

### THE NUMEROUS LINES OF RAILROAD

already built, or shortly to be constructed, and which have Grand Forks for a central and connecting point.

Of the roads to Crookston and Fargo we have already spoken, but there still remains to be mentioned the western extension of the Manitoba to Larimore, and the Devil's Lake country, and its northern route to the international boundary, near Pembina.  Both of these lines pass through and by numerous villages and towns, the trade of which, together with that of the surrounding country, is naturally tributary to Grand Forks.

Besides these branches of the Manitoba railroad system, a new road is to be constructed from Grand Forks to Columbia, Dakota, which will afford a competing line with the Northern Pacific to Chicago and the east. This is no paper road, but one on which construction has already commenced, and which a few months will see completed and in working order. At Columbia this road will connect with the Northwestern, over whose lines and connections freight can be shipped to any point in the Union.

HIGH SCHOOL.

THE PUBLIC BUILDINGS

of Grand Forks reflect the greatest credit on the enterprise of its people.  A splendid brick court-house, erected at a cost of $15,000, affords roomy accommodations for the various county offices.  A high school which cost $20,000, and which, for architectural beauty or solidity of construction, leaves nothing to be desired, attests the interest the citizens take in the great cause of public education.  There are, besides these, two more important buildings—a $5,000 city hall, and a $10,000 jail; this latter, however, is not yet completed, although the money has been voted and the contract let.  In this connection we must also mention the new water-works, which will supply the entire city with plenty of clear, good water, and the electric light shortly to be introduced. The grading and paving of the streets is being forwarded in a manner which sets a notable example to many older and more pretentious cities.

## THE STORES AND DWELLINGS

of Grand Forks are of the most substantial character; many of the most prominent professional and mercantile firms occupying handsome brick and stone blocks, a large number of which have been erected during · the present year. Perhaps the largest and handsomest business block in the city is that of the Citizens' National Bank, on the corner of Third street and Kittson avenue, a cut of which will be found on another page of this work. The building occupied by the First National Bank, on Third and Bruce streets, and another on Third street, between Kittson and De Mers avenues, and several others equally large and imposing, and all built of brick and stone, show that Grand Forks is rapidly becoming a city of no mean proportions, and one that is destined to become an important commercial metropolis in the near future.

In private residences, the splendid mansion of Captain Griggs, one of the earliest pioneers of the Red River Valley, and a gentleman who has always identified himself with the material progress of this city, is a dwelling-house which would be a credit to any large city. Its erection cost the Captain $15,000.

## THE RELIGIOUS DENOMINATIONS

are all represented by large and flourishing congregations. The Presbyterians, Episcopalians, Methodists, Lutherans, and Catholics have all fine churches; the last-mentioned denomination having just erected a large building on Sixth street, which is not yet completed. It is the finest church in Dakota, being 40x118 feet, brick veneered, and cost $18,000, all of which amount was raised in a short time by the members of the congregation, assisted by their fellow-citizens.

## SOCIALLY

Grand Forks leaves nothing to be desired. The population, though cosmopolitan in character, is made up of men and women of sterling character, industrious and persevering, who take the greatest interest in the development of their beautiful city. The Odd Fellows, Knights of Pythias, and other secret organizations count many members among the citizens. Near the city is located a fine driving park, where annually there takes place two or three days' racing, very liberal purses being offered, (this year $40,000,) and consequently the meeting draws together some of the finest horses in the Northwest.

### THE IMPORTANT MANUFACTURING ESTABLISHMENTS

are mentioned more at length further on in this work, so we shall only mention them briefly now.

The flouring mills, breweries, etc., are all doing a large business and adding greatly to the material wealth of the city. A foundry is soon to be started, and judging by the success that has attended the inauguration of similar enterprises in neighboring cities, it will speedily obtain all the business necessary to make it a splendidly-paying investment. A paper mill, which would convert into building paper the immense quantity of straw produced in the valley, would undoubtedly be very successful. This is an enterprise which would receive a most liberal support from the citizens, either in grants of money or land, and as the demand for building paper is very large, and there is only a single mill of the kind in northern Dakota, it could not fail to do a good paying business.

### A RECENT ASSESSMENT

of the taxable real estate and personal property of Grand Forks county, of which the city is the county-seat, gives for the latter $389,320 as the total personal; the principal items being: Manufactures, $7,999; merchandise, $172,050; horses, (numbering 218,) $20,445; cattle, (numbering 64,) $2,-360; money and credits, $58,400; stock and shares, $62,600. The total personal assessment for the county is $1,094,428,—an increase of $494,241 over the previous year; the principal items being merchandise and horses,—the former showing an increase of $109,578 and the latter $101,513. In real estate the increase in value has been equally as marked; the total county assessment for *lands* being $1,584,111 for 1882, as against $701,999 for 1881,—a difference of $882,112 in favor of the former year. The county acreage is placed at 269,498 in 1882, and 129, 327 in 1881,—a gain of 140,171 acres during the year. We should remark here, that government lands and those (homesteads and pre-emptions) on which the settlers have not yet proven-up and perfected their title, are not included in the foregoing. The taxable *lots* in the county number 5,681, and are valued at $1,000,582, of which lots 2,322 are in Grand Forks city, and are valued at $879,137. The following summary will show at a glance the wonderful increase in the value of taxable property of all kinds that has taken place in the county during the past twelve months:

SUMMARY.

1882.

| | | |
|---|---|---|
| Farming Lands, | - - - - - - - | $1,584,111 |
| City Property, | - - - - - - - - | 1,000,582 |
| Personal Property, | - - - - - - - | 1,094,428 |
| | | 3,679,121 |

1881.

| | | |
|---|---|---|
| Farming Lands, | - - - - - - $701,999 | |
| City Property, | - - - - - - 309,725 | |
| Personal Property, | - - - - - - 600,187 | $1,611,911 |
| Total gain, | - - - - - - - | $2,067,210 |

This splendid record of material progress is one of which Grand Forks has every reason to feel proud, since it is one equaled by few and excelled by none of the thriving cities and towns of the Northwest. Indeed, if we consider the *per centage* of increase—ONE HUNDRED AND TWENTY-EIGHT PER CENT.—*in one year*, it is an increase such as no other city in America can show.

While writing on this matter of taxation we may mention that the rate of county and territorial taxation is 12 1-5 mills on the dollar, divided as follows:

| | |
|---|---|
| Territorial, - - - - - - - - | 3 7-10 mills |
| County, - - - - - - - - | 2 " |
| Road and Bridge, - - - - - - - | 3 " |
| School, - - - - - - - - | 2 " |
| County sinking fund, - - - - - - - | 1½ " |
| Total, - - - - - - - | 12 1-5 mills |

Such, in brief, is the commercial history, present condition, and future prospects of Grand Forks, one of the most promising cities in Dakota. To the following pages we must refer the reader for more lengthy sketches of the principal business houses and industrial enterprises of the city, and for many interesting statistics useful alike to the merchant, capitalist, or professional man who desires to establish himself or invest his money among an enterprising, industrious, go-ahead people such as are the citizens of this, the METROPOLIS OF THE RED RIVER VALLEY.

# BANKS.

Grand Forks has three banking institutions, all possessed of ample capital, and doing a large and lucrative business. The rapid increase in size and importance of the city, the numerous new enterprises which are daily springing into existence, and the large agricultural country of which Grand Forks is the center, create a large demand for capital, which is sent in large quantities from the money centers of the eastern states for safe and well-paying investments in the real estate and commercial and industrial enterprises of the great west. In the following pages we give brief sketches of the principal banks, all of which are thoroughly reliable, being well and carefully managed by competent parties, most of whom have had a long experience in this business in the east.

## CITIZENS' NATIONAL BANK.

We mention this bank first among the financial institutions of the city, not only on account of its large capital and able management, but likewise because it is the successor of the pioneer bank of Grand Forks, which was one of the first banking houses established within the territory of Dakota. The original bank was known as the Bank of Grand Forks, and was controlled by very nearly the same gentlemen as those who are interested in the present organization. It continued as a private concern from September, 1879, until October, 1881, when the business had grown to such proportions, and its future seemed so secured, that it was resolved to reorganize as a national bank, under the name of the "Citizens'." Accordingly the capital was placed at $50,000, an amount which was speedily subscribed, and Mr. I. S. Eshelman was chosen president, and Mr. S. S Titus as cashier. The large and handsome brick building on the corner of Third street and Kittson avenue was used for the offices of the bank, and elegantly and comfortably fitted up. As a national bank its career of usefulness was materially extended, its deposits increasing until to-day they amount to considerably over $200,000. The Citizens' does a general banking and loan business, buys and sells foreign and domestic exchanges, and offers a sure and safe medium to distant parties for the transaction of all local financial business, such as the payment of taxes, purchase of real estate, or the making of collections, to which last branch of business the bank devotes especial attention. The Merchants' Bank of St. Paul is its correspondent in that city, while at Chicago it is connected with the Union National Bank. The gentlemen connected with the Citizens' are among the most prominent and influential citizens of Grand Forks, men who have largely contributed, by their enterprise and push, to placing this city on its present substantial footing.

## THE MERCHANTS' BANK.

Next in order of seniority to the Citizens' is the Merchants', a private banking house organized in the summer of 1881 by Mr. E. P. Gates, the capital of which is also $50,000.

Mr. Gates, when he first came to Grand Forks, was engaged in loaning money on real estate,—one of the safest and most profitable uses to which he could have possibly put his capital. The rapid growth of the tciy, and the increasing opportunities for investments which were daily occurring, led Mr. Gates to establish his bank as an easier method for the transaction of his business. The Merchants', like the Citizens', does a general banking business, its St. Paul correspondent being the First National Bank of that city. At New York it transacts its business through the Importers & Traders' Bank, one of the strongest financial institutions in the metropolis.

The Merchants' Bank also loans money as a first mortgage on improved or unimproved real estate, and Mr. Gates's long experience in this business enables him to conduct it most successfully.

He is a gentleman who enjoys to an eminent degree the respect and confidence of all who know him.

## THE FIRST NATIONAL BANK.

The growing size and importance of Grand Forks led some of its most influencial citizens to organize on the fourth of October, 1881, a national bank under the title of the First National. Mr. H. G. Stone was elected president and Mr. C. E. Burrell, cashier, offices they have continued to fill with credit to themselves and to the entire satisfaction of all interested, both stockholders and depositors, ever since.

That the public spirit which prompted its organization was duly appreoiated by those for whose benefit the institution was started, is shown by the fact that in less than a year of its existence its deposits already amount to thousands of dollars, and its orginal capital of $50,000 has been increased by a handsome surplus. A business which can show a record like this for its first business year, requires few words of praise. Its balance sheet speaks volumes for its able management, and the high esteem in which its officers are held by the community in which they live.

This bank, like the Merchants' and Citizens', does a general banking business; the First National Bank of St. Paul, Merchants' National of Chicago, and Merchants' National of New York, being its correspondents in the three cities named.

The directors have recently erected at the corner of Third street and Bruce avenue a substantial brick building, which the bank occupies. The structure is 24x60 feet, and cost $6,000; the interior fittings and furnishings being as handsome and commodious as those of any bank in the territory, and reflecting great credit on the public spirit of those who control the affairs of the First National.

# THE PROFESSIONS.

### LAWYERS, DOCTORS, AND REAL ESTATE DEALERS.

Under this title we include all who are not bankers, merchants, or manufacturers; the majority, it will be seen, being those engaged in the real estate business. It is one of the happy features of a young and prosperous community that there is very little litigation, and while the legal profession is represented at Grand Forks by many talented and able gentlemen, the amount of purely legal business is comparatively small. Land, the great basis of all real material wealth, is the great commodity dealt in by all classes in the west, and most of the lawyers are real estate brokers as well. The advantages that accrue from this are numerous and important. Most of the members of the legal profession have many acquaintances in the older states, who, relying on their knowledge, ability, and integrity, authorize them to act as agents for the investment of large sums of money, either as loans on real estate, or in its pur-

chase outright for investment and speculation. Thus much foreign capital
has been drawn to this section which otherwise would have never come
here, and the value of land, and the improvement of the city and country,
have been materially aided and advanced.

The doctors, while confining themselves more exclusively to their profession, are also mostly land-owners, many of them having considerable
capital invested in Dakota lands. To give some idea of the amount and
value of real estate transactions, as well as their growth and importance,
we have had prepared the following table, showing the warranty deeds
recorded in Grand Forks county for the two years ending September 1st,
1882.

While the list embraces all the warranty deeds that have been left for
record up to the time of its compilation, there are undoubtedly many
which have never been brought to the Record Office, and which, consequently, it was impossible to include. This is particularly the case as
regards the last few months, many deeds remaining unrecorded for months,
and even years, after their delivery.

This will account for the fact that for July and August in the present
year there is an apparent falling off in the number of deeds, although the
amounts are relatively as large. It is known that the sales of property
were very large during both of these months, but, as we have said, months
may elapse before the deeds are brought to the Record Office.

The totals and the increase, Grand Forks may well be proud of, for they
are larger than those of any city in northern Dakota or western Minnesota. Jamestown and Moorhead, on the Northern Pacific Railroad, whose
joint populations about equal that of Grand Forks, although the counties
of which they are the county seats contain 1,839,024 acres of land,
nearly a million more than Grand Forks, have 240 deeds *less* on record for
1881–82; a fact which clearly demonstrates which country is considered the better by the majority. of emigrants and new settlers.

2

# TABLE OF WARRANTY DEEDS

RECORDED IN GRAND FORKS COUNTY, DAKOTA, FOR THE TWO YEARS ENDING
AUGUST 31ST, 1882.

| MONTHS. | 1880–81 | | 1881–82 | |
|---|---|---|---|---|
| | No. | AMOUNT. | No. | AMOUNT. |
| September | 25 | $12,285 | 41 | $ 24,776 |
| October | 47 | 22,702 | 100 | 74,610 |
| November | 53 | 37,163 | 113 | 91,560 |
| December | 89 | 44,627 | 60 | 49,033 |
| January | 56 | 27,547 | 69 | 71,451 |
| February | 75 | 71,194 | 58 | 64,319 |
| March | 63 | 33,755 | 168 | 251,099 |
| April | 62 | 49,376 | 195 | 243,884 |
| May | 50 | 33,331 | 215 | 266,304 |
| June | 60 | 33,237 | 150 | 189,398 |
| July | 56 | 37,964 | 137 | 171,661 |
| August | 51 | 27,013 | 120 | 154,500 |
| Total | 687 | 430,194 | 1426 | 1,652,595 |

## BOSARD & CLIFFORD.

The senior member of this prominent legal firm is a native of Pennsylvania, and a graduate of the Mansfield Normal School in that state. After completing his studies in that institution, he entered the law office of Mr. Mortimer F. Elliott, the present Democratic nominee for congressman at large from Pennsylvania. Under that gentleman's direction he pursued a thorough course of legal study, and was admitted to the bar August 26, 1870, at Wellsboro, Pennsylvania, and for five years thereafter he was the law partner of his legal preceptor. In 1879, Mr. Bosard came west, locating at Grand Forks, and establishing himself with Hon. George H. Walsh, one of the pioneer attorneys of this section. During the first year, when Grand Forks was but a hamlet and the surrounding country but sparsely settled, and the legal business consequently limited, he was deputy register of deeds and deputy clerk of the district court, continuing, however, the practice of his profession.

Mr. George B. Clifford, the junior partner, is also an eastern man by birth and education. He is a graduate of Wesleyan Academy, Wilbraham, Massachusetts, and received his early legal training and instruction in the office of Hon. Roswell Farnham, the present governor of Vermont. In September, 1880, he was admitted to the bar of that state at Montpelier, where he remained until the following March, when, no longer able to resist the allurements of the new north-west, he came to Dakota. Very soon after his arrival in Grand Forks the present partnership was formed. In connection with their legal practice they engaged in the loaning of money on real estate and chattels, and having many friends in the east who placed with them funds for investment, they soon acquired a large and lucrative business. In March of the present year, in connection with several Vermont capitalists, they organized the Vermont Loan & Trust Company, of which Mr. J. H. Merrifield is the president and Mr. R. M. Sherman the secretary. Messrs. Bosard & Clifford then retired from active participation in the loan and real estate department of the business, devoting themselves entirely to their law business and the legal affairs of the company, for which they are the attorneys.

Their offices occupy the entire second story of the Citizens' National Bank building, and are as nicely finished and furnished, and they have as large and well-selected a law library, as any law firm in the territory.

These gentlemen, by their ability and large practice, have acquired a prominent place among the members of the Dakota bar.

### VERMONT LOAN & TRUST COMPANY.

In the previous article—that on Messrs. Bosard & Clifford—we mentioned the fact that this company succeed to the loan business of those gentlemen, and that it was organized in March—the 22d—1882.

Mr. J. H. Merrifield, the president, is from Vermont, as is also Mr. R. M. Sherman, the secretary, both of these gentlemen having removed to Grand Forks last March, just previous to the organization of the company. The Vermont Loan & Trust Company lends money in large or small amounts, on long or short time, and on either real estate or chattel mortgages. They are at present the agents for a large number of eastern capitalists who desire to invest their money where it is perfectly safe and yielding a much larger per centage then they could possibly obtain for its use in the Eastern states. It will not be inappropriate for us to say a word just here explanatory of the exceptional advantages which the west affords for making the very best investments. In the first place, land here is at bottom figures. The large quantities of government and railroad land to be had in various parts of this territory, at a comparatively trifling cost, and on long time, prevent the great inflation of prices which would be the undoubted result of the immense immigration which the country is receiving. While, however, the present figures are low, the near future will undoubtedly see a very rapid and substantial rise, as the country becomes more thickly settled and land scarcer. Hardly any combination of circumstances could occur to prevent the doubling in value of property in north Dakota within the next five years at least. Added to this fact—the present cheapness of land—there is the general prosperity of the people, and the prospect of immense crops, which will place, beyond a doubt, the borrowing class in a position to fully and promptly meet all their obligations.

We have dwelt at length on this matter of substantial security for money loaned to farmers and others in Dakota, because we believe it to be one which is only commencing to be thoroughly understood and appreciated by eastern capitalists.

No matter how good the security, however, the non-resident investor is obliged to rely mainly on the honesty, ability, and knowledge of his agents, and it is therefore important they should be responsible and competent parties. The Vermont Loan & Trust Company is composed of gentlemen of long experience in the real estate and loaning business, thoroughly acquainted with the value of property, and with the various laws and regulations controlling its transfer. They are loaning upon Dakota farms from $15,000 to $25,000 a month, and have had the best of opportunities to test by practical experience the safety and security of investments here. Loans made through this company net the lender eight to nine per cent. As it is well known here that these gentlemen have always on hand large sums for investment, they have daily applications for loans, and are consequently able to select the very best and safest investments offered. Eastern parties desiring to made safe and profitable investments of their capital, cannot do better than to enter into correspondence with this company.

## JOHN LAMB.

Mr. Lamb, previous to coming to Grand Forks, was for 11 years a resident of Minneapolis, Minn., where he was engaged in the practical pursuit of his profession, that of a civil engineer. While there he was engaged in designing many of the most important bridges and elevators on the line of the Chicago, Milwaukee & St. Paul Railroad west of the Mississippi river. Among these works we may mention, as evidences of his skill and ability as an engineer, the bridge over the Minnesota river at Chaska,

Minn., which is 250 feet in length, and another on the line of the Atchison, Topeka & Santa Fè road, a splendid structure, costing $30,000.

Mr. Lamb moved to this city in June of the present year and formed a partnership with Mr. W. D. Haycock, also of Minneapolis. But this latter gentleman having withdrawn from the firm, Mr. Lamb continues in his own name.

The importance of the business of a civil engineer cannot be overestimated in a country like this, where property changes hands so rapidly, where almost every day sees important additions laid out adjoining the principal cities and towns, and where the constant subdivision of large tracts of land into lots and small farms demand the constant services of a practical surveyor.

Mr. Lamb finds his time constantly occupied, and indeed it is with difficulty that he is able to attend to all the orders he receives for surveying and designing. As a practical evidence of his skill as a draughtsman and surveyor, we would call attention to the map of Grand Forks which accompanies this work, and which has been carefully lithographed from plats furnished by him. We are confident that it will be found the *best* map of this city yet published and we especially recommend it to the careful consideration of those who have not yet visited the city, but who are thinking of coming here to engage in business and to establish themselves as members of this prosperous community. By studying its general outlines they will readily understand the advantageous position which the city occupies on the Red River, and the systematic way in which it is laid out,—advantages which have materially aided in its growth and development.

Mr. Lamb, during the time he has been located in this section, has had an opportunity to study the chances for success that this country offers to the live, energetic man, and unhesitatingly says that he believes that any man of common ability and not afraid to work, can always make a living here, and if economical and saving can lay by something for the future at least.

## PARSONS & TEELE.

These gentlemen are among the most prominent real estate dealers in Grand Forks. Mr. Teele is from Illinois, and came west, locating at Moorhead, Minnesota, in 1880. There he was for some time the editor of the Daily *Argonaut*, but last March he removed to Grand Forks, and opened a real estate office in company with Mr. Cole. This latter gentleman, however, shortly afterwards withdrew from the firm, and Mr. Teele continued the business alone until last month, when he formed a partnership with Mr. Parsons. Their list of farming lands and town lots is the most extensive in the Northwest, and comprises over *twenty thousand acres*, a large portion of which lies in the famous Red River Valley, the most fertile and best wheat country in the world. They have some quarter (160 acres) sections and sections, every acre of which is susceptible of yielding over 25 bushels of the celebrated No. 1 hard wheat to the acre, and these they are offering on long time and at very low figures; much below the price which they will undoubtedly bring in a few months. Western people, believing that their true interests lie in settling up as rapidly as possible the vast prairies and fertile plains which characterize that section, prefer to sell on the most advantageous terms, so as to encourage immigration, rather than to retard it by waiting for high prices.

This explains the fact that improved farms can be obtained in Dakota for less than they would *rent* for in the eastern states or Europe.

To those who desire to engage in some commercial pursuit, in any of the various booming towns of the Red River Valley, Mr. Teele offers exceptional bargains in town lots for either business blocks or residences. He is the agent for Comstock & White, the owners of the town-sites of the thriving towns of Grafton, Minto, Manvel, Ardock, Hilsboro, Grandin, Fisher's, Sabin, etc. He has a personal knowledge of each of them, and can and will give full particulars to any one seeking information.

In Grand Forks he is the owner of one of the finest and largest addition to the city, and agent for Mr. A. Holes, in whose addition he offers 900 very desirable lots. He has also lots in McKelvey's and Budge & Eshelman's additions, and in the business center of the city.

ANDREW HOLES.

Although Mr. Holes is not a resident of Grand Forks, he has contributed so largely and so materially to its advancement and progress in wealth and prosperity, by investing large sums in city property, and by aiding in various ways in the development of its material interests, that any work descriptive of this city would be incomplete if it did not contain some mention of him. Mr. Holes is one of the original pioneers of the Red River Valley, one of those who, with true business foresight, foresaw the great and important position which this section of the United States was destined to occupy as one of the largest and best agricultural regions in America.

He came west over 10 years ago, before the Northern Pacific had laid its tracks to the Red River.  He was instrumental in securing the town-site of Moorhead for the Puget Sound Town-site Company, and has ever since been identified with the most important business interests of that city.

Guided by a long and practical experience, which enables him to forsee with accuracy the probable future of most of the new towns which are constantly springing into existence in the Red River Valley, he came to Grand Forks, which he knew was destined to be a *very* important point, looked over the ground and invested in a large tract of land, which he immediately proceeded to have surveyed and laid off into lots, and which is now known as "Holes's Addition."  A glance at the map which accompanies this work will enable any one, no matter how slight may be their knowledge of the plan of Grand Forks, to see at once that Mr. Holes selected his property with judgment, and that no more desirable lots are to be found anywhere in the city, especially when, besides their excellent location, the liberal terms on which they are offered for sale is considered. Mr. Holes is not one of those "penny-wise, pound-foolish" capitalists who are always waiting for a rise in the value of their property; he believes, and knows, that to successfully build up a new town, lots must be sold at a reasonable figure, one which will be sure to attract purchasers, and, although not a resident, as we have said, of this city himself, he still earnestly desires to see her prosper and grow, and proposes to aid this prosperity and growth by every means in his power.  With this aim in view he is offering his lots at very low figures, and has, consequently, disposed of many of them.  He still has on hand, however, a large number of splendid residence and business lots, and any one desiring to invest in Grand Forks real estate cannot do better than to address either him, personally, or his local agent, Mr. A. L. Teele, the real estate dealer, and editor of the *Golden Valley*.

### GRAND FORKS LAND & LOAN COMPANY.

The excellent opportunities for the making of safe investments, bearing a higher rate of interest than is obtainable in the east, which the Northwest offers, attracted the attention of several eastern capitalists, who organized a land and loan company, with an office at this point.  Mr. P. S. McGillivray, of Washburn, Ontario, a gentleman very well and favorably known through eastern and central Ontario for his business talents, being appointed manager.  Previous to opening their office here he made an extensive tour through North Dakota, familiarizing himself with the agricultural and commercial advantages of the different sections of the country.

On his return to Grand F'orks he decided to pay more attention to the handling of real estate than was first intended, and, with this end in view, associated with him Mr. W. D. McGregor, a gentleman whose experience in the real estate business and large connection throughout North Dakota made success in this line a certainty. Both these gentlemen are lawyers, and members of the Dakota bar.

This company has now on its books a long list of desirable farm lands and city property. It makes a specialty of transacting business for non-resident parties, such as buying property for speculative investment, loaning money on first mortgage, etc.

Those intending to come west to locate or invest, can, by entering into correspondence with this company, obtain full and accurate information and all particulars desired, thus avoiding the loss of time and expense incidental on a journey to the Golden Valley of the Northwest.

## BATEMAN & CHAMBERLIN.

sale and feed stable and veterinary infirmary, are in the center of the city, being on De Mers avenue, a few yards below Third street. Mr. Bateman, the senior partner, is from Port Perry, Ontario; Mr. Chamberlin is from Belvidere, Illinois. Both came to this city early in 1881. These gentlemen make a business of importing horses and mules, making a specialty of those most suited for the new settler or agriculturist, at the same time bringing in and having always on hand a few choice drivers and heavy draughts. From the fact of these gentlemen being veterinary surgeons and buying all their own horses, they are careful to buy none but sound animals. They have been nearly two years in business in this city, and it is good evidence of their success that they are arranging to erect a large new stable, which will be one of the best in the city. Parties in want of horses or mules will do well to give them a call before purchasing elsewhere, as they are both permanent and reliable. They have also a branch stable at Grafton, where they also do a large veterinary practice, which is conducted by E. L. Foy. Mr. Bateman being a graduate of the Ontario Veterinary College, Toronto, Canada, and having an experience of over ten years, is a sufficient guaranty that he is duly qualified to treat all diseases to which the horse, mule, or ox is subject.

The Messrs. B. & C. also make a speciality of examining horses as to soundness, and attend cases of all kinds both in town and country requiring veterinary skill, on the shortest notice, day or night.

## A. H. DE LANEY.

Mr. De Laney was a real estate dealer and sewing-machine agent, strange as it may seem to some of our eastern readers that any-one should conduct two branches of business seemingly so opposite as these.

When he first came to Grand Forks, in 1878, the population only numbered 800, and the railroad had not yet reached here. He opened a store and established himself as a machine agent. Gradually, however, he became interested in handling real estate and in making loans on well-secured mortgages. This branch of his business, at first of but slight importance, rapidly grew to large proportions, until to-day he is one of the most prominent real estate and loan agents in the city. Loaning money on well-secured real estate security may be considered as his specialty, and having been, comparatively speaking, one of the earliest settlers, he is thoroughly acquainted with the value of property, and consequently knows at once exactly how much money can be safely lent on it. To parties in the eastern states, who have large or small sums which they desire to invest where the rate of interest is higher, while the security is equally as good, as in the older sections of the country, Mr. De Laney offers his services as one thoroughly competent to act as their agent in making all such investments. Land here is as low as it is ever likely to be, even in times of panics or great financial distress, so the security offered is certain not to depreciate in value. Besides, there is another point in favor of the safety of western investments, and that is, that western people, if not more honest, certainly show themselves much more willing to pay their debts, strange as it may seem to those who know nothing of this section or its people, except what they have gleaned from sensational reports about Indians and desperadoes.

When Mr. De Laney's real estate business grew to such large proportions, he resolved to relinquish his sewing-machine interests, so as to devote himself entirely to the former occupation. Accordingly, he recently disposed of all his stock and fixtures, and the entire sewing-machine business, and now has no connection with it.

He is a gentleman who enjoys, to an eminent degree, the esteem of all who know him.

## ELDER & CO.

Among the professional firms of Grand Forks none rank higher than Elder & Co., although they are among the most recent acquisitions to the professional community.

Mr. Elder is from Iowa, where he was engaged in his present business, so that he came to this city thoroughly competent to attend to all its details. He at once made himself acquainted with the city and surrounding country, and speedily obtained the agency for the sale of a large amount of town property and desirable farming lands. He shortly afterwards associated himself with Mr. W. A. Selby. This latter gentleman is a lawyer by profession, a graduate of a prominent Pennsylvania law school, in which state he practiced for some time after his admission to the bar. On coming to Grand Forks he devoted himself more particularly to practicing before the United States Land-Office. He attends to all land contests, final proof papers, etc., and has had an extensive and very successful experience.

Perhaps no firm in the city has more complete or larger lists of property for sale than Elder & Co. They have lots in every addition to the city, either improved or unimproved, farms at various points in the Red River Valley, and are able to offer many very desirable bargains.

It often happens that parties intending to come West desire to enter into correspondence with some thoroughly reliable real estate agent, who can place them in the way of obtaining the class of property they desire before coming out themselves. By this means they are enabled, by dealing through a broker or agent, to have their farm or house all prepared and selected for them when they arrive, thus enabling them to commence business immediately on their arrival. This, when practical, is a very wise and judicious plan, and is to be greatly commended. Messrs. Elder & Co. are prepared to act in this way for any of their customers, and thorough and complete reliance can be placed in their judgment and reliability. All who are thinking of emigrating to this fertile and prosperous region can obtain from this firm all the information needed, and plats and full descriptions will be sent them, by which to select their purchases themselves, if they so prefer. Both the members of the firm are well known to the citizens of Grand Forks as square-dealing, public-spirited business men.

## H. P. WILLSON & SON.

The senior member of this prominent real estate and insurance firm is from Wabasha county, Minnesota. He is by profession a lawyer, having pursued a long and careful course of legal study at Wabasha, in which town he also practiced for several years after his admission to the bar. Being attracted to Grand Forks by reason of her superior business advantages, he, in the early spring of 1881, opened an office in this city, in partnership with his son, Mr. Frank A. Willson.

Here he relinquished the practice of his profession, (with the exception of appearing before the U. S. Land Office,) devoting himself entirely to dealing in real estate, and the placing of loans on improved and unimproved property, in which he has been very successful.

Land here is as low as it is ever likely to be, even in times of panics or great financial distress, so the security offered is certain not to depreciate in value. The profits derived from farming and merchandising are so large that the borrower, if engaged in either business, is almost sure to be able to pay the interest regularly.

All that is needed, therefore, is an honest, competent agent, who will attend faithfully to the safe placing of the loan, the collecting of the interest, and the return of the principal when the time expires.

Mr. Willson possesses, as we have already shown, both the legal knowledge and practical experience to act as agent for any eastern parties desiring to invest either in this city or surrounding country. He says that any amount of money could be safely placed in this section at not less than seven per cent.

He has already transacted business of this character for large numbers of non-residents, and always with the most satisfactory results.

Mr. Frank A. Willson devotes himself exclusively to the insurance branch of their business, which is very large, as they have the exclusive agency at this point for several of the largest companies in the country, among which we may mention the New York Life, with a capital of $46,000,000, the Home Fire Association, Phœnix, Continental, etc., the total capital of which aggregates $43,000,000.

These gentlemen rank among the foremost professional firms in the city, being indorsed by some of the most prominent public and business men of the Northwest.

LEWIS LAMB.

Mr. Lamb conducts a real estate office on De Mers avenue, just east of the Griggs House.

He is from New York, and came to this city in February, 1882. Although a comparatively recent acquisition to the ranks of the professional community, Mr. Lamb has been very successful as a real estate dealer, and has now on his books one of the largest lists of town and country property of any broker in the city. His improved and unimproved farms, situated in various parts of the country, are adapted to almost any class of agricultural pursuits. The new-comer desirous of buying and locating in this favored region cannot do better than, on his first arrival, to examine this list of property, and he will find Mr. Lamb willing and glad to assist, to the utmost of his power, in obtaining just the character and description of farms desired.

Much valuable time is not unfrequently wasted and serious mistakes made by parties who, instead of availing themselves of the experience and knowledge of others, prefer to follow their own ideas, without having the slightest acquaintance with the country or its advantages. All this might be avoided if recourse was had to a thoroughly reliable land agent like Mr. Lamb, in whose office may be found maps, plats, and a complete description of all the lands he has for sale.

He enjoys a reputation for business ability and square dealing second to none in the city, and makes a specialty of transacting business for distant parties by correspondence.

JOHN ZERFASS, JR.

This gentleman makes a specialty of city real estate, although he is also the agent for a large amount of out-of-town property. His office is on De Mers avenue, just west of the Griggs House. To merchants and business men, who propose to remove their establishments to Grand Forks, or to those who desire to engage in any industrial enterprise, Mr. Zerfass's lists of city property offer many desirable bargains, and it would be of advantage to those persons to place themselves in communication with him, as he can undoubtedly be of much service in advising them.

Having a thorough knowledge of the city he is specially qualified to handle town property, and many of the best located lots in the city for business purposes are under his control. He also has a list of desirable

residence lots in the best residence part of Grand Forks, and these he is prepared to sell on the most liberal terms.  He guarantees satisfaction in all
business transacted by him, and has made many important sales, some of the
best property in the city passing through his hands.  He will gladly answer
all letters of inquiry concerning Grand Forks and its vicinity.

--◆--

# MANUFACTURERS, MERCHANTS, ETC.

We have already spoken in our opening sketch of the important commercial position Grand Forks occupies at the confluence of the Red and
Red Lake Rivers.  We have noted the fact that she is undoubtedly destined
to be an important manufacturing and mercantile center,—the distributing
point for the surrounding country.  That her manufactures are as yet undeveloped, or comparatively so, is evident when we remember that the city
is of such recent growth, and that a large manufacturing center takes time,
money, and untiring industry to build it up.  Still she has already her flour
mills, manufacturing a superior grade of flour from the famous "No. 1
Hard" wheat, in the growth of which the surrounding country is so pro-
lific.  She has breweries, saw-mills, boat-yards, carriage and wagon fac-
tories, and good prospects of a foundry and paper-mill at no distant day.
But these are the mere pioneers of the large manufactories of which she
shall one day be the seat.  As the country which surrounds her settles up,
as her own population increases, as, above all, the numerous lines of railroad and canals which will connect her with other large industrial centers
are completed, she will gradually rise into a large, substantial, and important manufacturing city.

Her wholesale jobbing trade, as yet only a commencement, is rapidly
becoming larger and more extensive, and needs only time to make it an
important factor in her future greatness.

## LUKE, STEELE & CO.

There can be no more important and useful business in a new and rapidly growing agricultural community, like that of the Northwest, than dealing in farming implements, and the gentlemen who have the agencies for the leading manufacturers invaribly have a very large trade. Luke, Steele & Co. are the local agents for the Buckeye mower and reaper, harvester and self-binder, Sweepstakes threshers, and Monitor engine, besides handling the Lake City wagon, Hoosier seeder, Hollingsworth and Tiger hay-rakes, and Deere plows.

The members of the firm are Messrs. D. W. Luke, W. N. Steele, and P. N. Trahn, gentlemen of large experience in dealing in farming machinery. The firm also carries a full line of general hardware, stoves, tin-ware, glass, nails, etc.

The principal office is at Grand Forks, but the firm has branches at Grafton and Minto, two thriving Dakota towns, on the Manitoba railroad, not far from this city.

The business of the firm for the last year has been very large and satisfactory, and they are about to erect a handsome brick building, 50x100, on the site of their present agricultural warehouse.


## E. TAYLOR & CO.

This firm established themselves in the retail grocery business in this city during the past summer, purchasing the property which they now occupy for that purpose. Their store is on Third street, in a central and eligible locality, convenient to both the resident and business portions of the city. They make a specialty of fancy groceries, pickles, and fine teas and coffees. It may be well to remark that it is specialty stores of this kind—stores which confine themselves to a single branch of business, as groceries, dry goods, clothing, etc.—which distinguish Grand Forks from the majority of western towns, marking her distinctively as an important business point; for it is only where the population is large, and trade extensive, that a classified business can exist. In small towns, the stores are mostly of the general merchandising class—dry goods, groceries, etc., being sold by the same firm or establishment.

Messrs. Taylor & Co. have had the satisfaction of finding their business venture rewarded by a marked success.

## BROOKS BROTHERS.

It can be readily understood that in a country like this, where each day adds its hundreds, and often thousands, to the population, no business can be more important than that of dealing in building materials. Houses are alike a necessity to the farmer, the merchant, and the traveler, and shelter is always the first object of the solicitude of the new settlers.

Brooks Brothers' is one of the oldest and most reliable firms engaged in the lumber business in Grand Forks, where they have established for themselves an enviable reputation for their square dealing, and the thorough business principles which characterize all their transactions.

## JULIUS SILL.

Among the recently established business houses we may mention that of Mr. Sill, who is the proprietor of a dress goods and millinery store.

His stock of ladies' goods is very large and well selected, and offers to the fair sex of Grand Forks an opportunity for purchasing all they need without the necessity of sending to the larger cities. This is an advantage which the ladies will not be slow to avail themselves of, as shopping by letter must certainly lose many of the fascinating qualities which belong to the system of personally visiting the stores and examining the goods.

Mr. Sill intends to spare no pains to keep his establishment fully up to the demands of his customers and the needs of a rapidly growing community.

## M. W. SULLIVAN.

The wholesale and retail liquor store of which Mr. Sullivan is the genial proprietor, is on East Third street near the post-office.

His establishment is one of the best in the city. It is fitted up in a neat and attractive style; the stock of choice wines and fine liquors is one of the largest and best-selected in Grand Forks, and the bar and fixings are handsome and substantial. Mr. Sullivan is among those enterprising business men who have already made endeavors to obtain for Grand Forks a portion of that wholesale jobbing trade which she is undoubtedly destined to acquire in the near future. While giving his personal attention to all the details of his retail business, he is gradually enlarging and extending his jobbing trade, and already has met with the most gratifying success.

Mr. Sullivan entertains the highest opinion of the future of the city, and considers it as a business point second to none in the Northwest, especially in the golden valley of the Red River.

Besides his liquor business he is also a wholesale and retail dealer in cigars, and carries a large stock of the finest brands. He does a large and satisfactory business, which is rapidly increasing.

## DAVIS & CANNIFF.

The members of this enterprising firm of house, sign, and carriage painters are gentlemen of great experience in that line. Mr. Canniff came to Grand Forks from Kingston, Canada, where he was engaged in business. He is, however, a native of England, and brings to his present occupation a thorough and practical knowledge of all its requirements.

His partner is also a practical painter of long experience, and a thorough master of his trade.

Being practical workmen, they personally supervise and manage all work intrusted to them, and employ only skilled help to assist them.

Besides painting, they take orders for frescoing, kalsomining, graining to imitate all the various kinds of wood, gilding, glazing, and paper hanging. They carry a large and well-selected stock of wall paper, and do a large business in this line. They make a specialty of imitating marble, and specimens of this class of work executed by them show that they thoroughly understand the business.

Their orders are so numerous that they are kept constantly busy, and are forced to employ some seven or eight men to help them.

## WILLIAM BUSSE.

Mr. Busse devotes himself to administering to the wants of the inner man by keeping a first-class confectionery and ice-cream parlor, as well as by conducting a first-class bakery, known as the " Palace Bakery."

He is from St. Paul, but has been a resident of Grand Forks for some time.

Good bread is one of the great requisites for the enjoyment of perfect health, and, in supplying the citizens with an A. 1. article, Mr. Busse has found his reward in obtaining one of the best customs in his line in the city.

3

His establishment is fitted up in the neatest style, and everything about the place is clean and inviting.

His stock of confectionery, fruits, and nuts is large and fresh, and he exerts himself to satisfy all the demands of his patrons.

## M. RUETH.

The establishment of which this gentleman is the genial proprietor is known as the "Red Front Grocery." It is located on Third street, in one of the most central localities in the city.

This gentleman carries a full line of staple and fancy groceries, teas, coffees, and canned goods, of which he makes a speciality; his stock being the largest in the city. His goods are all fresh and well selected, especially the fancy groceries, and he aims to keep constantly on hand a full supply of everything needed by his numerous customers. He has consequently acquired one of the largest and finest customs in his line in the city.

Mr. Rueth is from Cold Springs, Stearns county, Minn., where he was formerly in business. He came to Grand Forks and established himself in this store in last March, and at once took rank among the most enterprising and public-spirited citizens.

## T. RICE.

Cleanliness being next to godliness, laundries should be valuable aids to us on our road to heaven, and Grand Forks is certainly very fortunate in having such a well-conducted establishment of this kind as that over which Mr. Rice presides.

The Cascade Laundry is on Third street, between Alpha and De Mers avenues, opposite the Commercial Hotel, a central and convenient locality. Mr. Rice, the proprietor, is a gentleman who has had a long and practical experience in this business, and he conducts his laundry in a manner which places it at the head of anything of the kind in Dakota.

He makes a specialty of fine work, which he does up equal to new, and has consequently secured the patronage of a large number of the prominent citizens of Grand Forks.

## JOHN J. McCALLUM.

In the spring of 1879 Mr. McCallum opened a merchant tailoring establishment in this city, a branch of business which had previously been greatly neglected.  He purchased a large stock of cloths, cassimeres, etc., and, being a practical tailor of long experience, he soon obtained an extensive custom, which has ever since been on the steady increase.  Indeed, the clothing made by this gentleman compares, in elegance of style and neatness of fit, with anything turned out by the best eastern establishments.  He has the patronage of all those who desire a fine suit and a good fit in the city, besides a large country trade, parties coming to him frequently from a distance to make their purchases and leave their orders.

## M. WITTELSHOFER.

Mr. Wittelshofer is proprietor of the finest jewelry store in Grand Forks.

He is a gentleman who has had a long experience in his present business, and when, in the Fall of 1880, he came to this city and opened his present establishment, he speedily obtained a large and lucrative trade.

He makes a specialty of repairing watches and jewelry, and in this department of his business he has been especially successful in his efforts to please his customers.  His stock of jewelry, silver and plated ware, watches, etc., is very large and well-selected, and exceeds in variety of styles and novelty of design that of any similar establishment in the city.

Mr. Wittelshofer takes great interest in the development of the material interests of Grand Forks, and speaks in the highest terms of the city's advantageous location for commercial and industrial business of all kinds. As an evidence of this he cites his own experience, his sales having so greatly increased during the past few months that he has been obliged to remove from his old store to his present large and commodious quarters.

## H. & E. THARALDSON.

These gentlemen conduct a general merchandising establishment. Their store contains a large and complete assortment of dry goods, notions, boots, shoes, clothing for men and boys, hats, caps, ladies' dress goods of all kinds, table and household linen, staple and fancy groceries, and a miscellaneous assortment of everything in the dry goods and grocery line.

Everything has been selected with the view of supplying *all* the demands of a large and growing trade, and the quality and prices are as various as the tastes and pockets of the purchasers.

The proprietors are from Norway, but have been living and doing busi-· ness in this country for several years. They enjoy a large custom, and are patronized by the majority of their co-patriots, who make up no inconsiderable portion of the enterprising, industrious citizens of this section.

## C. ANDERSON.

The need of competent wagon and carriage makers, in a city surrounded like this by so large an agricultural population, is evident at the first glance; and Grand Forks is fortunate in possessing a gentleman who has had a long and practical experience in the business, and who is a thorough master of it. We refer to Mr. C. Anderson, who came to this city in the spring of 1880, from Red Wing, Minnesota, of which place he had been the pioneer wagon and carriage maker.

He also attends to horse-shoeing, in which branch of business he has acquired one of the best runs of custom in Grand Forks, the farmers coming from the surrounding country to patronize him.

He has a paint-shop connected with his factory, so that he is able, not only to make, but to paint and finish carriages.

He thinks Grand Forks one of the best business points he knows of.

## P. T. McQUILLAN.

This gentleman is the proprietor of a retail wine and liquor establishment on Third street, next door to the Merchants' Bank. The stock of wine and liquors is very large and well selected, everything being of the best and purest in the market.

There are several billiard tables of the very best make, handsome bar and fixtures, and everything is conducted in the best style and most orderly manner.

As Mr. McQuillan's establishment is one of the most centrally located in town, in the very heart of the business section, near the intersection of the two principal streets, (Third street and De Mers avenue,) and convenient to all the larger hotels, he does a very large business, and speaks in the highest terms of the promising future of Grand Forks.

## C. L. BAKER.

The business conducted by this gentleman embraces everything in the grocery, provision, and crockery line. Besides a complete assortment of the staple articles usually found in a store of this kind, Mr. Baker keeps constantly on hand a full line of fancy groceries, sauces, crackers, essences, etc. The central position of Grand Forks, connected by numerous railroad lines with all the growing towns of the Red River Valley, is such that she is rapidly becoming a distributing point for the surrounding territory, and her jobbing trade has already assumed no mean proportions. Mr. Baker and his fellow merchants are doing all they can to encourage the establishment of this wholesale trade by offering large stocks of goods at low prices. Mr. Baker makes a specialty of this branch of business, and is rapidly gaining a large jobbing trade. He is also an extensive dealer in teas, of which he handles the largest stock in Grand Forks. He is an enterprising, energetic business man.

## HARRY BEYER.

Mr. Beyer came to Grand Forks in February, 1881, from Emerson, Manitoba, and established himself at once as a first-class, practical painter. The rapid growth of the numerous towns and cities in the Northwest, and especially of places of the size and importance of Grand Forks, has created an immense demand for mechanical labor of all kinds, and while even the poorest workmen find plenty to do, those who are thoroughly masters of their trade at once find themselves in the greatest demand, and in a position where their skill and knowledge will command the highest remuneration. This is the case with Mr. Beyer, and it is not surprising to learn that every moment of his time is fully occupied attending to the numerous orders he is constantly receiving for work from those who need the services of a first-class painter. Many of the new and handsome buildings recently erected in Grand Forks owe a large part of their interior decorations to his skill, and bear evidence to the fact that he thoroughly understands his business.

## HALEY & LESTER.

Among the recent acquisitions to the business community of Grand Forks is the firm of Haley & Lester, tinners and repairers, whose store is on De Mers avenue, near the freight depot.

These gentlemen are from Le Sueur county, Minnesota, where they were engaged in their present occupation. They removed to this city in May last, and shortly after arriving opened their present establishment, speedily acquiring a very good trade.

Having a practical knowledge of their business, and an extensive experience, they personally attend to the manufacturing of their tin-ware, of which they carry a large and well selected stock.

In repairing they are kept constantly busy, and indeed find it frequently very difficult to fill all the orders they receive.

With a present business so large and so rapidly increasing, these gentlemen have every prospect of a successful business future.

## A. W. SMITH.

One of the most important industrial establishments in the city is the Red River Flour and Saw-mill, owned and operated by Mr. A. W. Smith. The superior quality of Red River Valley wheat, and its peculiar adaption to milling, has made the flour of this section world famous, and that produced by this mill is remarkably pure and white.

The large pineries in the adjacent state of Minnesota, and the easy means of transportation afforded by the rivers which unite at Grand Forks, makes this an excellent point for the establishment of saw-mills, and Mr. Smith does a very large lumber business.

## GRAND FORKS BOAT YARD.

This is another important local industry, and one that has contributed materially to the city's growth and advancement. The yard was established in 1871 by Mr. N. W. Kittson, of St. Paul, who placed it under the charge of Mr. D. P. Reeves. It afterwards passed under the control of the Red River Transportation Company, who at present control it.

## S. SWENNUMSON.

Nowhere, if we except perhaps the railroad and telegraph, has American genius been more remarkably displayed than in the wonderful machinery it has invented to aid the farmer in the work of cultivating the soil and gathering his crops.

Improvement follows improvement so rapidly in this department of mechanics, that what to-day seems unsurpassable, to-morrow will be antiquated, and we shall doubtless not rest until we have a combined harvester, thresher, and mill.

Although we have not yet reached this last stage of perfection, the Osborn favorite agricultural machinery, for which Mr. Swennumson's is the local headquarters, is wonderful, not only for the mechanical ingenuity displayed, but likewise for its wonderful adaptation to all the various farming operations.

Mr. Swennumson is from Jacksonville, Iowa. He has traveled extensively through the Northwest, selling horses and cattle, and has had an agricultural experience of over 20 years. He established himself here last spring, and has already done a very large business, which gives every promise of greatly increasing in the near future.

## JOHNSON & ANDERSON.

These gentlemen are wholesale and retail dealers in crockery and glass-ware,—the only exclusive merchants in this line in the city.

The senior member of the firm (Mr. Johnson) has for many years been engaged in this branch of business at 513 Washington avenue south, Minneapolis, and a little over a year ago, seeing the growing importance of Grand Forks, he, in company with Mr. Anderson, opened a store in this city. Their stock, which is very large and well selected, embraces china-ware, including bed-room sets in numerous varieties and styles, breakfast, dinner, and tea sets, many of them of beautiful designs, table cutlery in great variety, stone-ware, of which they have a large assortment, looking-glasses and mirrors, lamps of all sizes and shapes, vases, plated and willow wares, pictures, frames, glass-ware, etc.

Mr. Anderson is the local representative, and to his good judgment and business ability the firm owes the major part of its success. The firm is already doing quite a jobbing trade, which is being rapidly extended and gives every promise of being very large in a few years.

## GAHR & DOBMEIER.

We must not omit to mention the Grand Forks brewery, of which these gentlemen are the proprietors, as it is one of the most important manufacturing establishments in the city. The senior partner is from Germany, where he was engaged in his present occupation before coming here, so that he brings with him a large experience, which has been of material benefit to him in the making of his present business a success. The brewery has a capacity of 4,000 barrels annually, all of which is sold in the city or surrounding country.

## WILLIAM SHANNON.

Mr. Shannon is from Canada, and shortly after his arrival in this city he opened a first-class carriage and wagon factory and repair shop. Being a thorough mechanic, and understanding his business in all its details, he speedily obtained a very satisfactory custom, which has been on the steady increase ever since.

Speaking of the advantages this country offers to persons in this trade, Mr. Shannon says that they could not be better, as work is plenty and remunerative.

## FITTER BROTHERS.

These gentlemen came to Grand Forks, the one from St. Louis and the other from New York, over two years ago, and established themselves as dealers in groceries and provisions. They built the large store (22x52) which they now occupy, at the corner of Third street and International avenue, one of the most central localities in the city. Here they carry a very large stock of staple and fancy groceries and provisions. Their trade is not confined to the city, but extends over much of the surrounding country, embracing many important towns. They are among the most successful merchants in the city.

## FRANK ROFF.

Mr. Roff conducts a large livery and sale stable, where he keeps constantly on hand a fine stock of riding and driving horses, buggies, carriages, and road wagons for hire, and also horses and mules for sale.

He is from Rochester, Minn., but has been established in his present business here for some time.

The demand for teams and vehicles is very large at a point like this, where dozens of land seekers are daily arriving to inspect the surrounding country, and Mr. Roff finds a well-paying business in supplying transportation to his numerous patrons. Indeed, the difficulty is to find accommodations for all, and not unfrequently he is taxed to the utmost to meet the demand. He, however, spares no pains to keep not only a large stock but also a good class of horses and carriages, and visitors or those in search of land cannot do better than to obtain their teams from him.

## E. F. LUMBARD.

Mr. Lumbard is proprietor of the city bakery, besides conducting a confectionery and grocery store.

His bakery is the largest in the city, his trade embracing not only Grand Forks, but also much of the surrounding country. In the manufacture of his bread he uses only the best and purest flour, made from the famous No. 1 hard wheat, and as a result it is as fine and white as possible.

He does a very large and satisfactory business, which he is rapidly extending by his industry and push.

Having had a long and practical experience with horses, he is of invaluable service to those desiring to purchase working stock for their farms, and in his stables will be found at all times a fine collection of animals specially adapted to farming purposes. He makes it a rule to deal squarely with every one, and can guaranty the soundness of all horses or mules sold by him.

This is of great importance, especially to the inexperienced buyer, and is an advantage of which he should not fail to avail himself.

## JOHN STEWART.

Mr. Stewart is the proprietor of a grocery store on De Mers avenue, formerly owned by Mr. F. M. Crandell, but which the former gentleman purchased a little over a year ago, since when he has continued to manage the business himself.

He carries a fine and extensive stock of coffees, teas, sugars, pickles, canned goods, and, in a word, a complete assortment of staple and fancy groceries. By strict attention to business he has acquired a large trade, which he is continually increasing and extending.

## J. CUMMINGS.

To shoe a horse as it should be done is an art which requires experience to acquire, and although there are many blacksmiths professing to understand the business, there are few who are really masters of it. Mr. Cummings is one of these few, and has, consequently, one of the largest customs in this line in the city. He came from Canada to Grand Forks in March, 1881, and shortly after arriving here commenced business. It was not long before his superior abilities were discovered, and he acquired a large trade. Although horse-shoeing is his specialty, he does all kinds of blacksmithing, repairing, etc. His business for last year shows a very gratifying increase, and a good promise for the future.

## J. W. WORKS.

Mr. Works is from Maine, and came to this city in February, 1882, shortly afterwards opening a large sale and livery stable on De Mers avenue, between the Griggs House and Mansard House hotels. He buys and sells horses, oxen, mules, etc., and does a very large and extensive business. His livery stable is first class in every respect, and he is at all times prepared to supply teams and guides to parties desirous of visiting the surrounding country, either as land-hunters or simply on pleasure trips.

The demand made on him for teams and conveyances of all kinds alone amounts to very large proportions, especially during the spring and autumn, when the rush is the greatest; and as the majority of the newcomers become farmers, they necessarily create a large demand for stock of all kinds. It is therefore not surprising to learn that the business of this gentleman already reaches very large figures, and that it gives every indication of rapidly increasing in the near future.

## JACOB BERG.

Among the earliest business establishments to locate in a growing western town there is almost invariably a photograph gallery, probably because the settlers are fond of sending home photographs of themselves and their homes. Mr. Berg cannot lay claim to having been a pioneer of Grand Forks, since he has only been here a little over one year, but in his particular line he was one of the first to locate here. He came from Minneapolis, where he had been employed at his present business with John Olsen, a photographer of that city. Having had a long and thorough experience, his work shows every evidence of the care and ability with which it is executed.

## O. BARQUIST

This gentleman came to Grand Forks in January of the present year, and shortly after his arrival he opened a retail liquor establishment on Fourth street. He carries a large stock of fine wines, whiskies, liquors, etc., and his place is fitted up in a neat and tasty manner, while the whole business is conducted quietly and orderly. Mr. Barquist is from Wabasha county, Minnesota, where he was engaged in business. He speaks most encouragingly of the future of this city, pronouncing it the most substantial city this side of St. Paul and Minneapolis.

## BROWN & SON.

The members of this hardware firm are Mr. W. H. Brown and Mr. F. A. Brown, his son, both of whom have had a long experience in their present business, as their store, established in 1877, was the pioneer hardware store in Grand Forks.

These gentlemen carry a large and full stock of general and building hardware, blacksmith supplies, sashes, doors, building paper, etc. They make a specialty of the celebrated "Charter Oak" cooking-stove and "Argand" base burner, both coal stoves. They are also manufacturers of tinware, of which they keep on hand a fine assortment, and take orders for sheet-iron work, which they execute in the most satisfactory manner.

They are doing a large trade, and consider Grand Forks a splendid business point.

## REED & CO.

Among the more recent establishments in Grand Forks, we must mention that of Messrs. Reed & Co., retail dealers in wines, liquors, and cigars, whose place is on East Third street, near the agricultural warehouse ofSeymour, Sabin & Co. They have a very large stock of imported brandies, old whiskies, fine wines and liquors, all of the purest and best brands to be found in the market.

Their saloon is tastefully and elegantly fitted up, everything being as neat and comfortable as paper, paint, and good fixtures and furniture can make it.

The proprietors are from Wisconsin, but were persuaded to remove to this city by the reports of its fine business prospects. Since their arrival they have enjoyed a very fine custom, and are satisfied that they made a good move in coming here.

## STEWART & SUTLIFF.

These gentlemen are blacksmiths, who, having had a long and practical experience in the business, are prepared to do all kinds of work in their line in the most satisfactory manner, and at very reasonable rates. They have only been established here during the present year, yet they have already acquired a large business, and are meeting with the success their skill and ability deserves.

## T. E. DAVIES.

This gentleman is the proprietor of a store on Third street, where he keeps a stock of fruits, candies, liquors, etc. He came to Grand Forks from Winnipeg, the capital of Manitoba, a city which has been "boomed" to a great extent during the last two years. That Mr. Davies should have left there to go into business in this city, is an evidence that he, at least, considers this the better and more substantial business point of the two,—a conclusion which the future will most likely prove to have been correct. Places which spring suddenly into size and importance are likely to experience an equally sudden collapse while those which, like Grand Forks, grow rapidly, but at the same time substantially, retain their size and importance. Mr. Davies is doing a good business, and has every reason to feel satisfied with the change.

Grand Forks is well supplied with hotels and boarding-houses, yet they are all doing a very large business, and not unfrequently it is difficult to find accommodations.

## THE GRIGGS HOUSE.

This is the largest hotel in the city. It is located on De Mers avenue, near the business portion of the city. It is a large three-story brick-veneered building, with accommodations for over one hundred guests.

The present proprietor is Mr. C. B. Ingalls, a gentleman who has been very successful in its management.

## THE MANSARD HOUSE.

The proprietor of this hotel is Captain Maloney, an old pioneer, who erected the first part of his hotel in 1874.

The Mansard is a large and commodious house, well-kept, with good meals, and clean, neat bed-rooms, and does a very large business.

## COMMERCIAL HOTEL.

This first-class hotel is located on Third street, at the intersection of Alpha avenue, near the business center of Grand Forks. The house is new throughout, having been erected the past spring by the proprietors, Messrs. Ryan & Crowley, expressly with the view of its adaptation to its present purposes.

The building has a frontage of 50 feet on Third street, by a depth of 70 feet, with a large kitchen in the rear. The office and sample room are each 24x22 feet, while the dining-room is 24x42 feet. The house is two stories high, with a mansard roof, and contains 32 elegantly furnished bed-rooms.

The proprietors, understanding that comfortable sleeping apartments and good meals are no less requisite to the success of their hotel than a new house and furniture, have devoted themselves specially to these matters, and having had a long experience in hotel keeping, as the proprietors of the *Red River Valley House*, they have succeeded in at once placing their house in the front rank among the hostelries of Grand Forks.

Mr. H. P. Ryan is from Ottawa, Canada, and Mr. C. Crowley from New York. The former came here some two years ago, and was shortly followed by his partner.

## THE NORTHWESTERN HOTEL

is the oldest hotel in the city, the building having been erected for this purpose by the Hudson Bay Company, in 1874. Mr. P. Carroll is the present proprietor, who takes a pride in keeping his house up to the highest standard of excellency.

## THE VIETS HOUSE.

This is another first-class hotel, kept by Mr. W. B. Dow. He sets an excellent table, and has comfortable bed-rooms and large sample-rooms for commercial travelers. Mr. Dow can accommodate about 75 guests.

## THE RED RIVER HOUSE.

This is a small hotel, but none the less neat and clean. It is located on De Mers avenue, north of Third street. Mr. Joseph Dennis is the proprietor, a gentleman who does his best to please his guests, and succeeds so well that his house is always full. He sets a good, substantial, table, has neat, clean bed-rooms, and charges more moderate prices than some of the other hotels.

## A. KNUDSON.

Mr. Knudson keeps a Scandinavian hotel, which is very largely patronized by his co-patriots, who form a considerable portion of the industrious, hard-working population of this section. His house is clean and neat, and the comfort of the guest is the object of the continual solicitation of the proprietor, who personally attends to the management of the whole house.

## L. LEMBECK.

Mr. Lembeck is the proprietor of a boarding-house. He is from Cold Spring, Minnesota, and established himself in his present business in this city last June. He has a large house, sets a good table, and does his best to merit the large patronage he enjoys.

# THE NEWSPAPERS.

Grand Forks is well supplied with newspapers, both daily and weekly. The *Herald, Plaindealer*, and *News* publish daily and weekly editions, while the Scandinavian citizens have a weekly called the *Tidende*. The *Golden Valley* is particularly devoted to the interests of land seekers and those seeking information concerning the Red River country.

## THE HERALD.

The editor of the *Herald* is Mr. Geo. B. Winship, formerly proprietor of the Caledonia *Courier*, published at Caledonia, Houston county, Minn.

He removed here several years ago and started the *Herald* as a weekly. His paper meeting with marked success, he, on the first of November, 1881, added a daily edition.

The daily is a four-page, seven-column sheet, ably edited, containing all the associated press dispatches, special telegrams, and much local news, while the weekly is a condensation of the daily editions, with much new and interesting matter added. Its circulation approaches 1,500, and is rapidly increasing.

There is a large job printing office and book bindery connected with the *Herald*.

## THE PLAINDEALER.

Mr. W. J. Murphy is the present proprietor and editor of this, the oldest newspaper in Northern Dakota, the first number having been issued in 1875. The *Plaindealer* contains full telegraphic reports from all parts of the world, together with much local news. Its editorials are spicy and well written, and it is a credit alike to its editorial management and the city. It publishes a daily and weekly edition.

## THE NEWS.

The *News*, though a younger claimant on popular favor, (its first daily edition bearing the date June 25, 1882,) yields nothing to its older cotemporaries in the amount of news it furnishes, nor the ability displayed in its editorial columns. Messrs. Hansbrough & Briscoe are the proprietors and managers. The paper is independent republican in its sentiments.

### THE TIDENDE.

This newspaper has a very good circulation among the Scandinavian settlers in the Valley. It is ably edited, and contains all the news.

### THE GOLDEN VALLEY.

Mr. A. L. Teele, formerly editor of the Moorhead *Argonaut*, conducts the columns of the *Golden Valley*. The special object of this paper is, as we have said, to afford information to those seeking to obtain a correct idea of the Red River Valley, and the agricultural, commercial, and industrial advantages it offers. It is a paper which should be in the hands of every one proposing to come west, and we strongly recommend those who propose to remove to this section to send for copies, which will be cheerfully sent on application.

# CONCLUSION.

We give below a table showing the number of establishments in Grand Forks and the number of their employes, together with the amount of business done by them during the year ending September 31, 1882. Also the increase under each of these heads as compared with the year ending September 31, 1881:

COMPARATIVE BUSINESS STATEMENT

For the Two Years Ending September 31, 1882.

| KIND OF BUSINESS. | Establishm'ts. | Increase. | Employes. | Increase. | Amount of Business. | Increase. |
|---|---|---|---|---|---|---|
| Agricultural Implements......... | 9 | 3 | 35 | 9 | $ 465,000 | $ 246,000 |
| Bakers and Confectioners......... | 6 | 2 | 18 | 5 | 46,000 | 20,000 |
| Bankers.................... | 3 | .. | 9 | 2 | .......... | .......... |
| Barbers..................... | 4 | 1 | 11 | 3 | 8,400 | 2,500 |
| Blacksmiths and Wheelwrights.... | 8 | 3 | 26 | 11 | 33,000 | 16,000 |
| Brick-yards ................... | 4 | .. | 65 | 25 | 45,000 | 20,000 |
| Butchers .................... | 2 | .. | 8 | 3 | 44,000 | 20,000 |
| Clothing Dealers, (Dry Goods, Boots, Shoes, Hats, etc.,).............. | 14 | 5 | 42 | 18 | 417,000 | 255,000 |
| Contractors and Builders.......... | 15 | 4 | 130 | 31 | 550,000 | 200,000 |
| Doctors and Dentists............. | 12 | 5 | 18 | 8 | 10,800 | 3,200 |
| Druggists..................... | 4 | .. | 12 | 2 | 25,000 | 12,300 |
| Furniture and House Furnishing Dealers...................... | 3 | 1 | 10 | 4 | 54,000 | 24,000 |
| Grocery, Flour, and Feed Dealers.. | 14 | 5 | 56 | 21 | 560,000 | 200,000 |
| Hardware Dealers and Tinsmiths.. | 5 | 1 | 21 | 5 | 125,000 | 25,000 |
| Hotels and Restaurants.......... | 10 | 3 | 96 | 22 | 121,247 | 37,247 |
| Jewelers..................... | 5 | 1 | 13 | 5 | 15,500 | 4,500 |
| Laundries.................... | 3 | 1 | 10 | 8 | 8,000 | 3,500 |
| Lawyers..................... | 15 | 5 | 22 | 9 | 17,000 | 8,000 |
| Livery and Sale Stables.......... | 5 | 2 | 27 | 9 | 112,341 | 26,000 |
| Lumber Dealers................. | 9 | 2 | 31 | 18 | 217,000 | 67,000 |
| Painters..................... | 4 | 1 | 10 | 3 | 27,000 | 13,000 |
| Printers and Publishers.......... | 5 | 2 | 22 | 13 | 35,000 | 13,000 |
| Real Estate Dealers............. | 23 | 9 | 31 | 15 | 1,500,000 | 837,000 |
| Surveyors and Architects......... | 3 | 1 | 5 | 2 | 12,000 | 5,000 |
| Unclassified*................. | 3 | .. | 18 | 3 | 56,000 | 16,000 |
| Wines and Liquors.............. | 12 | 5 | 26 | 12 | 63,000 | 26,200 |
| Totals................. | 197 | 61 | 776 | 256 | $4,567,288 | $2,095,447 |

* "Unclassified" embraces the following branches of business: Brewery, Cigar Factory, and Boat Yard.

4

## POST-OFFICE.

The following interesting statistics were furnished us through the kindness of the postmaster, Mr. D. McDonald:

| | |
|---|---:|
| Amount received from M. O., year ending July 1, 1881, - - - | $29,826 73 |
| "     paid on          "        "        "     " - - | 15,927 85 |
| "     received from  "        "        "  1882, - - - | 45,738 32 |
| "     paid on          "        "        "     " - - | 28,364 55 |
| Total receipts from sale of stamps, etc., 1881, - - - - | 5,256 25 |
| ".         "         "         "     1882, - - - | 7,923 87 |

| | |
|---|---:|
| Estimated No. pieces mail matter forwarded, 1881, - - - - | 365,000 |
| "         "         "         "  1882, - - - | 620,000 |

D. McDONALD, P. M.

## THE UNITED STATES LAND OFFICE.

The business of the United States Land Office at Grand Forks having grown too large for the limited accommodations it previously occupied, its offices have been recently enlarged, and it now occupies the entire second floor of Gotzian's block, 22x80 feet.

The receiver, Mr. W. J. Anderson, has prepared the following summary of all business transacted since the opening of the office, April 20, 1880, up to October 1, 1882.

### SUMMARY.

| | Acres. |
|---|---:|
| 6,328 Homestead entries, embracing, - - - - - | 984,298.23 |
| 4,425 Pre-emption filings, embracing, - - - - | 708,000.00 |
| 2,386 Timber-culture entries, - - - - - - | 379,756.12 |
| 385 Soldiers' declaratory statements, embracing, - - - | 61,300.00 |
| 4,421 Cash entries, embracing, - - - - - - | 691,083.95 |
| 403 Excess receipts, embracing, - - - - - | 3,180.51 |
| 154 Final proofs, - - - - - - - - | 18,609.94 |
| 13 M. B. land-warrants, - - - - - - - | 1,800.00 |
| Total receipts of the office, - - - - - - - | $982,854.89 |

## POPULATION.

Nothing we could possibly say would show more plainly the rapid development and increase in population of this section than these figures. The homesteads alone, placing the number to a family at five persons, gives an increase in population of THIRTY-ONE THOUSAND SIX HUNDRED AND FORTY in less than THIRTY MONTHS, or at the rate of over ONE THOUSAND per month. And this, be it remembered, is the increase in the *country*, entirely independent of the hundreds and thousands who have taken up their domiciles in the various towns and cities.

Since the first part of this work was written the line of the St. P., M. & M. Railroad, on the west side of the river, has been completed to the international line, giving direct communication with Winnipeg and the Canadian Pacific road.

The Duluth and Winnipeg, a new opposition line passing through Grand Forks, and which will very likely be under the control of the Grand Trunk Railroad Company, is being pushed to completion, and the Minnesota & Dakota Northern, a line running north from Moorhead and the Northern Pacific, is also being rapidly laid. The western extension of the St. P. M. & M. is being pushed towards the Devil's Lake country, a section destined to be of immense agricultural importance. A new telegraph line to connect with the south and Minnesota is being rapidly constructed.

It is exceedingly difficult to correctly estimate the population of a city growing as rapidly as Grand Forks, but from a carefully-collected census we think it is about SIX THOUSAND.

At an election held on the first of September last, 386 votes were cast in the city and 111 in the country; the vote being on the question whether the county should be bonded for $10,000 to build a jail. As we have already noticed, it was very largely affirmative. The bonds were sold at a good premium, showing conclusively that the credit of the county is most excellent.

Situated so advantageously on the borders of a large navigable river, in the center of a splendid agricultural region, connected by numerous lines of railroad with all sections of the country and the northwestern British provinces, Grand Forks has before her a future second to no other city in Dakota. Her citizens are industrious and energetic, and propose to keep her in the future, as she has been in the past, at the head of the commercial and industrial cities of this section. They intend that she shall ever be the METROPOLIS OF THE RED RIVER VALLEY.